# The Adventures of

# HARRY

# the 60-Pound Guard Cat

## By

## Roger Breternitz

Harry was not like any cat most folks would ever know or be able to pet.

Harry was a 60 pound Canadian Lynx. Some people call them Bobcats, but they are totally different animals.

They are very dangerous in the wild or their natural surroundings, but Harry was friendly as could be and would even let you pet and play with him!

Harry was a very special cat. Not a house cat, nor a fat cat, nor a rat cat...Harry was a GUARD CAT!

Cats are very strong animals for their size and very quick, but Harry was 4 times as strong as any house cat, and faster that lightning!

Sometimes Harry would even let one of his friends carry him around when he felt in a lazy mood.

Harry lived on a very beautiful boat called a yacht. It was docked in a marina in a city called Marina del Rey in California. There were many yachts in the marina, but his was one of the biggest and most beautiful. Harry loved his yacht.

It was Harry's job to guard and protect this beautiful yacht, and guard he did. He was always watching for unwelcome visitors.

Harry thought, "Of all the types of animals my owner could pick to guard this boat, I'm just the right one. I'm strong, fast, small enough to get around secretly, and I work cheap!

Harry thought to himself, "The cockpit has a good view, I'll just station myself here as a lookout for a while."

"I think I'll get to know these controls a little better," Harry told himself.

"You never know when the Captain might want me to pilot the boat in case of an emergency."

Soon Harry thought, "I'd better continue making my patrol rounds, and check below deck.

Silently he crept down the stairs, his paws barely touching the fine carpet. Harry knew how to take care of things and not let his sharp claws catch on the carpet or furniture.

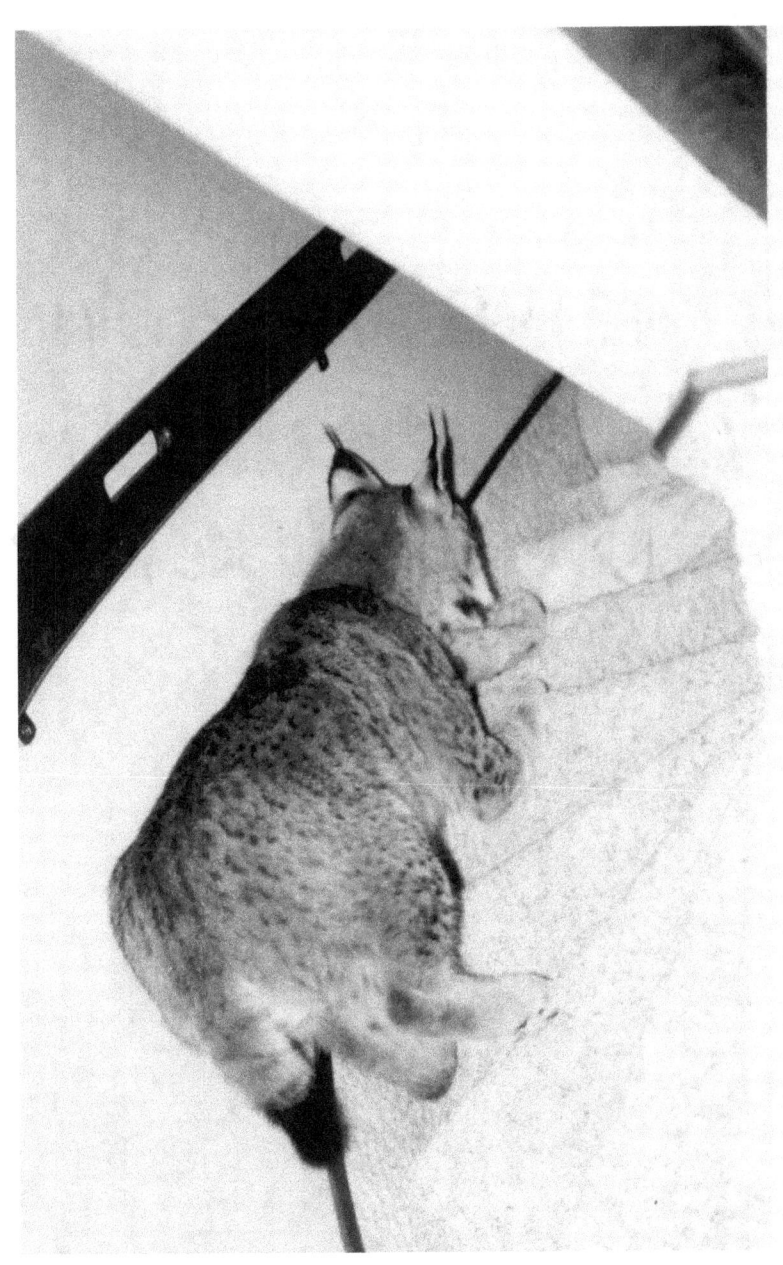

"This towel looks a little crooked," Harry thought, as he adjusted it with his paw. "I like to see things neat, clean and in order."

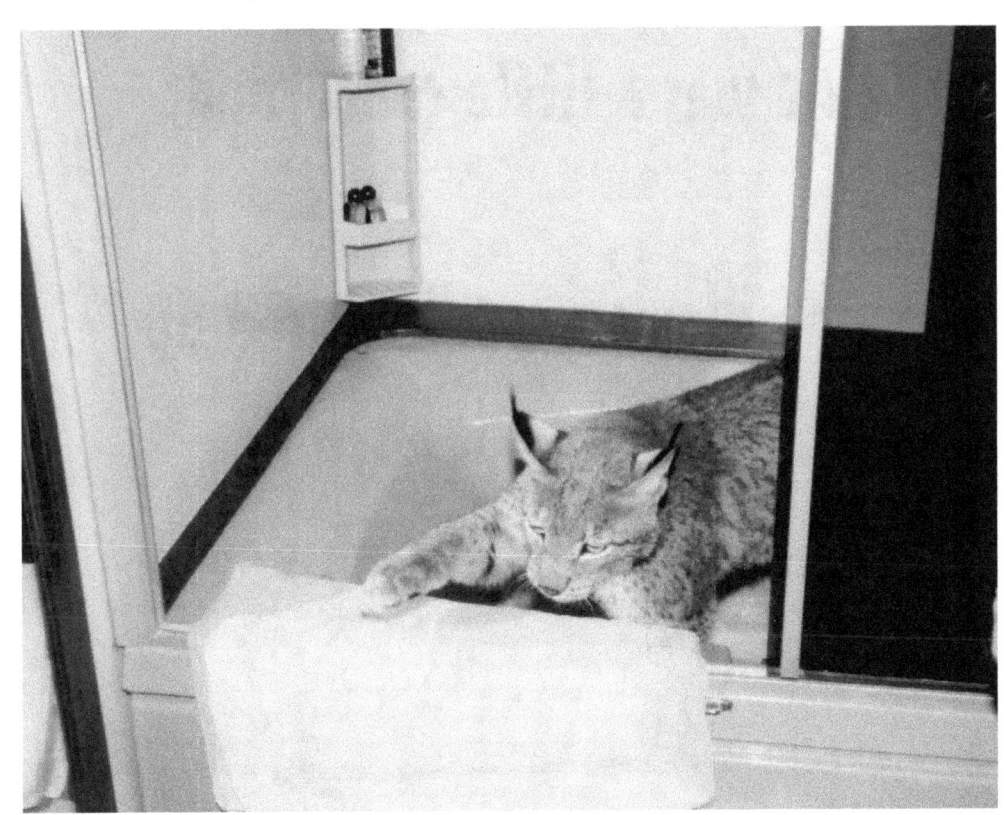

When Harry got to the Captain's suite he was a little concerned,

"These pillows are all messed up," he told himself. "I'll have to rearrange them to get this room ship-shape."

Suddenly Harry made a real find!

"This is my blanket I've been looking all over for!" he exclaimed. Harry loved his blanket, and was very happy he found it.

"MMM, My," he thought. "I guess my blanket got washed with that great smelling softener, I'll just take a little break for a while."

Harry dozed off for a few minutes with is favorite blanket. "It doesn't get any better that this," he thought to himself.

Suddenly Harry woke up and realized, "Hey! Wait a minute, I've got things to do and places to be!"

"Not so fast," Harry said to himself. "I've made a mess of this bed. I can't leave without straightening the covers."

Harry always cleans up any messes he makes and keeps things in order, because he cares and has a sense of responsibility to everyone around him.

As Harry looked at his job of making the bed he thought "There, it's not perfect, but a great job for a guard cat with more important things to do with his time."

I need some exercise," thought Harry, "I think I'll work out with my tennis ball to keep my teeth sharp.

Harry loved his tennis ball, and had put lots of holes in it with his sharp teeth.

"I think I'll exercise my jaws for a while with my favorite ball," thought Harry.

"This tennis ball work-out stuff takes a lot energy, I feel like I could use a short nap," thought Harry.

Just as a nap gives us energy so we can have more fun later, Harry needed a nap to keep him sharp for his patrol duties.

"Let's see," thought Harry, "I need a long flat place in the middle of the boat, and not too soft." Harry didn't want to sleep for very long because he still had rounds to make.

"Here's the perfect spot," thought Harry to himself. The table was just the right size for him.

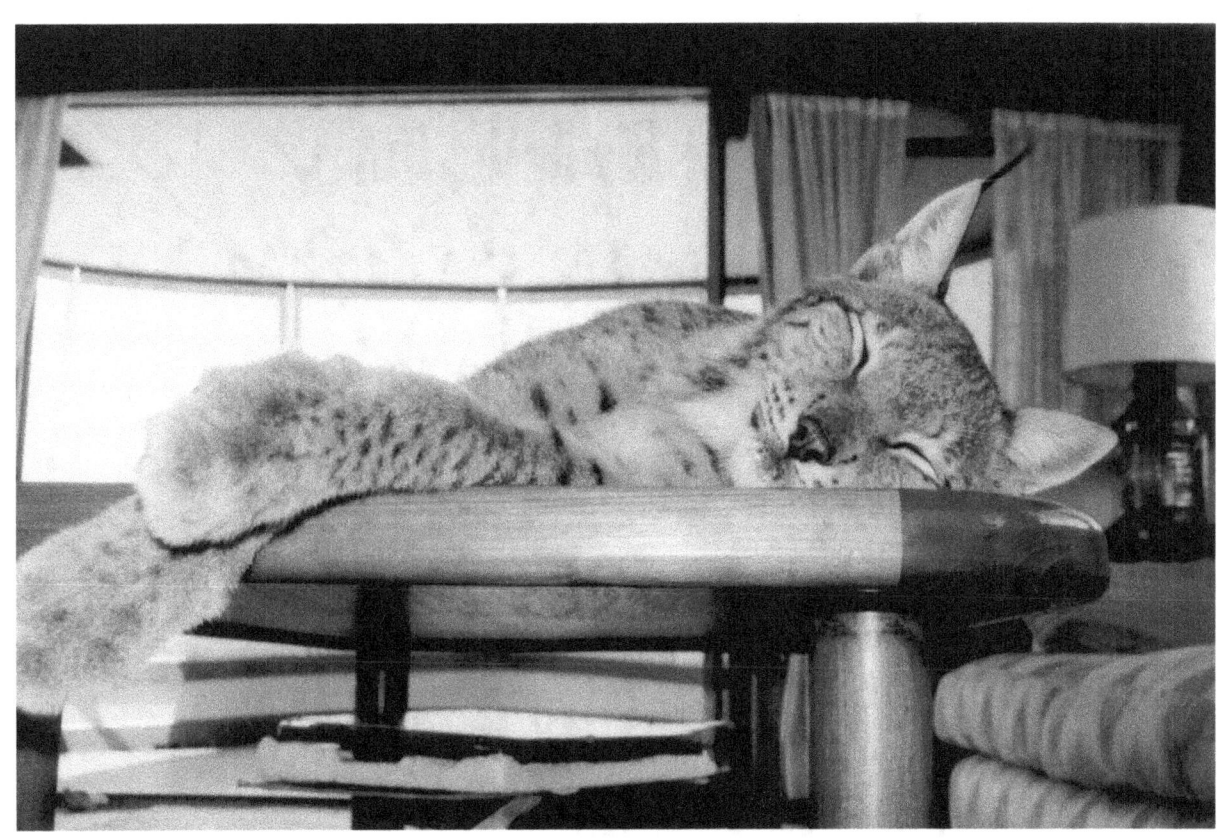

Soon Harry was fast asleep, dreaming of chasing a big bully of a dog, snapping at his hells. Harry really scared him, and the dog had to jump over a high fence to barely get away.

"Take that," thought Harry. "That's for all the cats of the world."

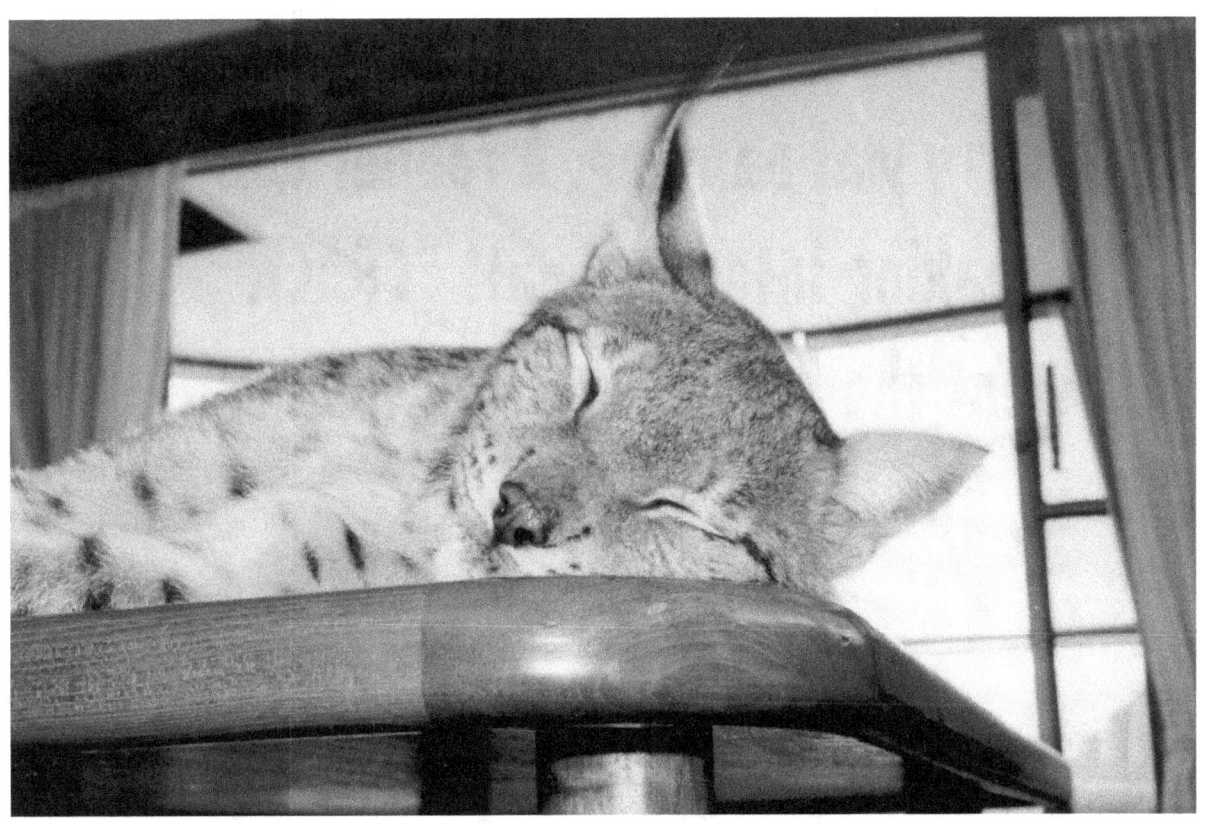

Something was happening while Harry was napping. A robber was breaking into the boat! "CRACK" went the lock as he tried to break in, but the door was stuck.

The thief was a tuff one, not about to give up!

"What's that sound?" thought Harry as he was jolted out of his dream. "Something's wrong," he told himself.

Suddenly Harry was wide awake and ready to move!

He raised his head to listen better, because he knew something was not right. "I need to go take a closer look," he told himself.

# Harry ran to the window!

The robber was just getting the door open, and thought he'd really hit the jackpot!

He didn't know what trouble he was in for, because...

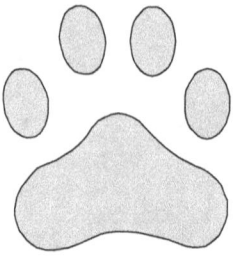

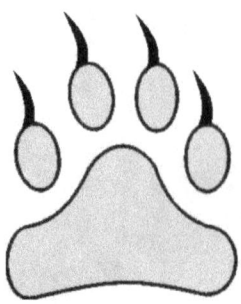

# Harry was watching!

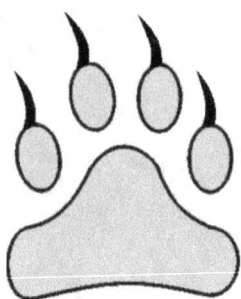

Harry crept silently around the back of the couch, under the end-table, and waited with his claws out for the thief to pass by.

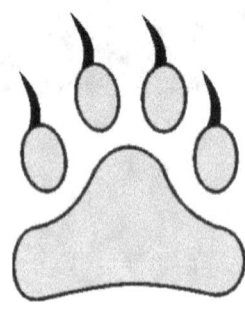

Harry crouched like a steel spring, waiting for just the right instant when this loser would pass by.

He was ready to pounce with all his might! When the burglar walked by, Harry sprang through the air like a bolt of lightning!

# The burglar turned around just in time to see Harry, but it was too late!

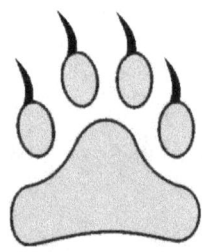

Harry knocked the thief to the floor, and was on top of him in a second! The guy knew he was in big trouble!

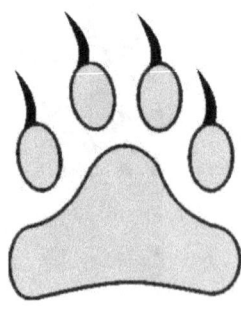

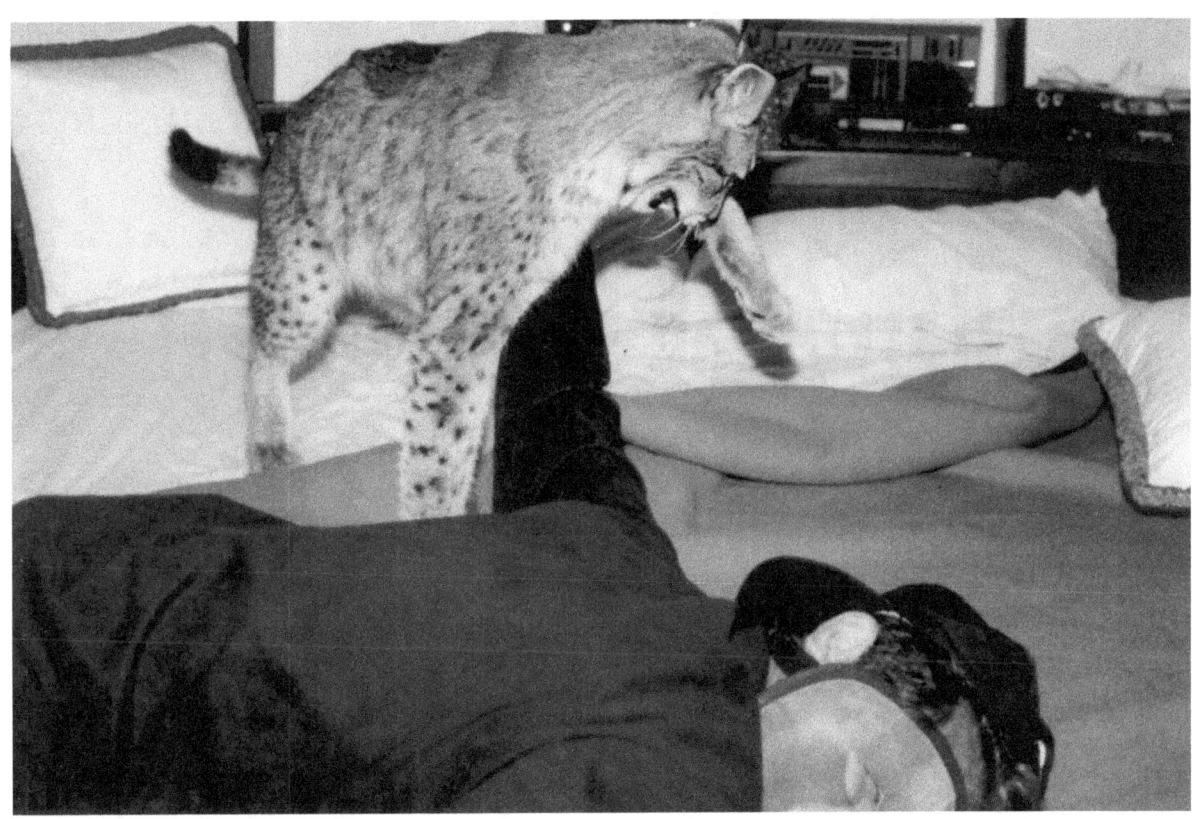

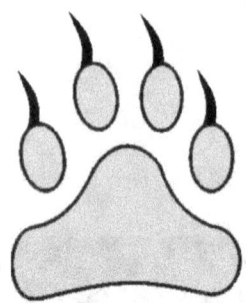

# Harry had him pinned down, and wouldn't let him up.

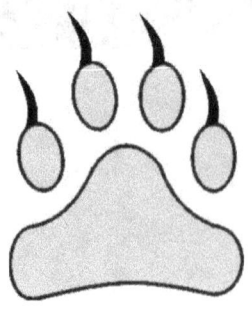

"I'll grab him here," thought Harry, as he wrapped his paws around the robber's arm.

The robber screamed in terror, "No! I promise, I'll never rob anyone again!"

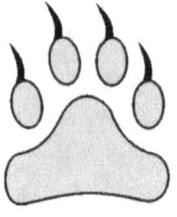

Then Harry went to work on the crook with his back feet and claws. "Take that, you loser," thought Harry.

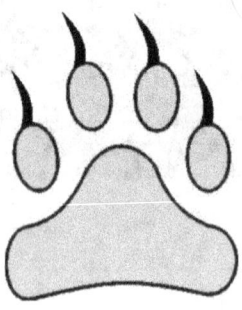

Finally the robber could hardly move, but had enough strength to try to crawl away. "Not so fast," thought Harry, "How about a bite out of his leg here!"

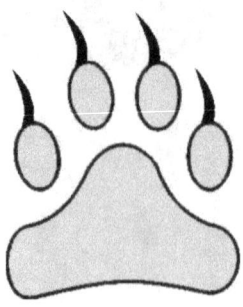

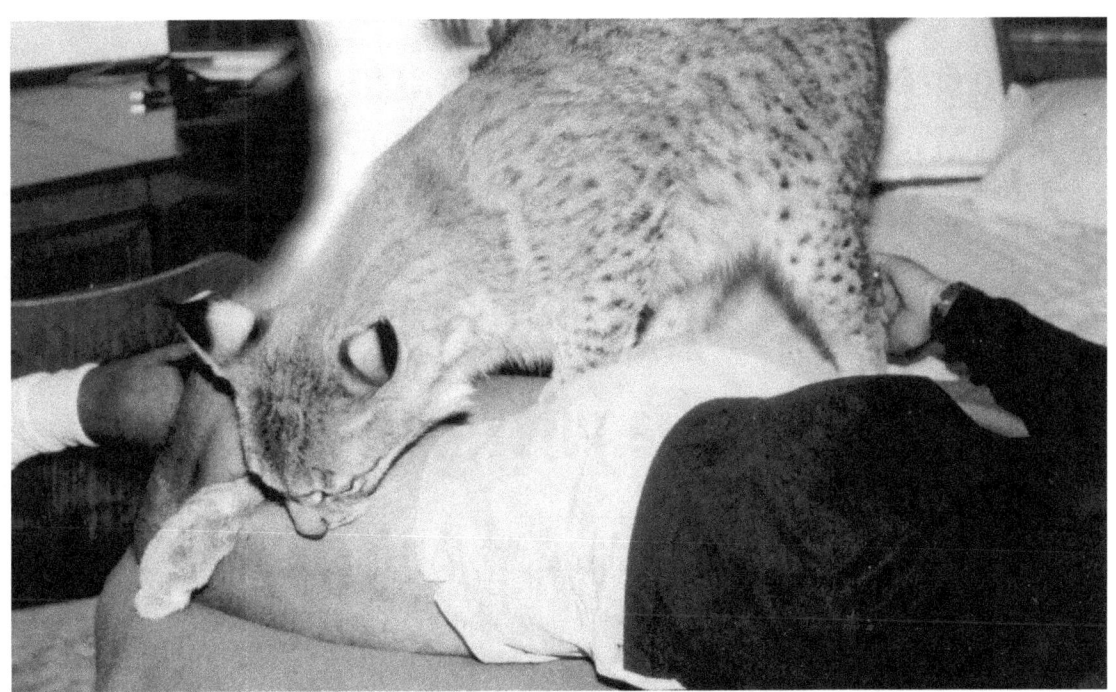

The robber didn't care how cold the water was, or how deep the water was, or even if he could swim or not. He just knew he wanted off that boat and away from Harry.

The robber was terrified! He knew if he didn't get off this boat, he was in REAL trouble!

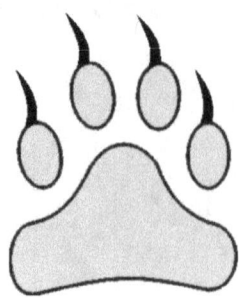

Just as the robber was trying to swim away, the Harbor Patrol happened to be going by. The Sheriff recognized the thief from the reports.

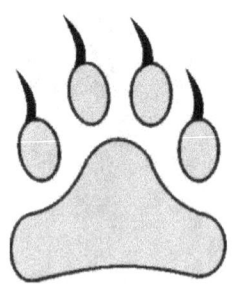

The Sheriff's deputy whirled the boat around and came back as fast as he could. He said, "Good work Harry, we've been looking for this guy for weeks!"

They put the hand-cuffs on him and took him off to jail, where he is still behind bars to this day!

There was a large reward for this thief. The next day a very nice lady from the Marina Protection Society came by a presented Harry's owner with a big check for the reward.

The Sheriff even made Harry an honorary deputy for doing such a good job. Everyone was very proud of Harry!

"What a day," thought Harry. "I saved the boat, scared off a robber, and captured a big reward! I should become a private eye! Maybe I'll do that tomorrow, but right now I need a nap."

So Harry stretched out on the Captain's bed where he wasn't allowed, but no one told him to get down. They knew he deserved a rest.

Sure it was a tough day, and Harry was really tired, but don't think you've seen the last of. . .

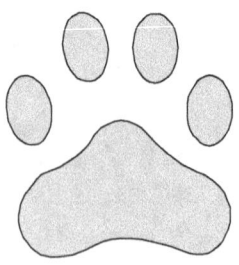

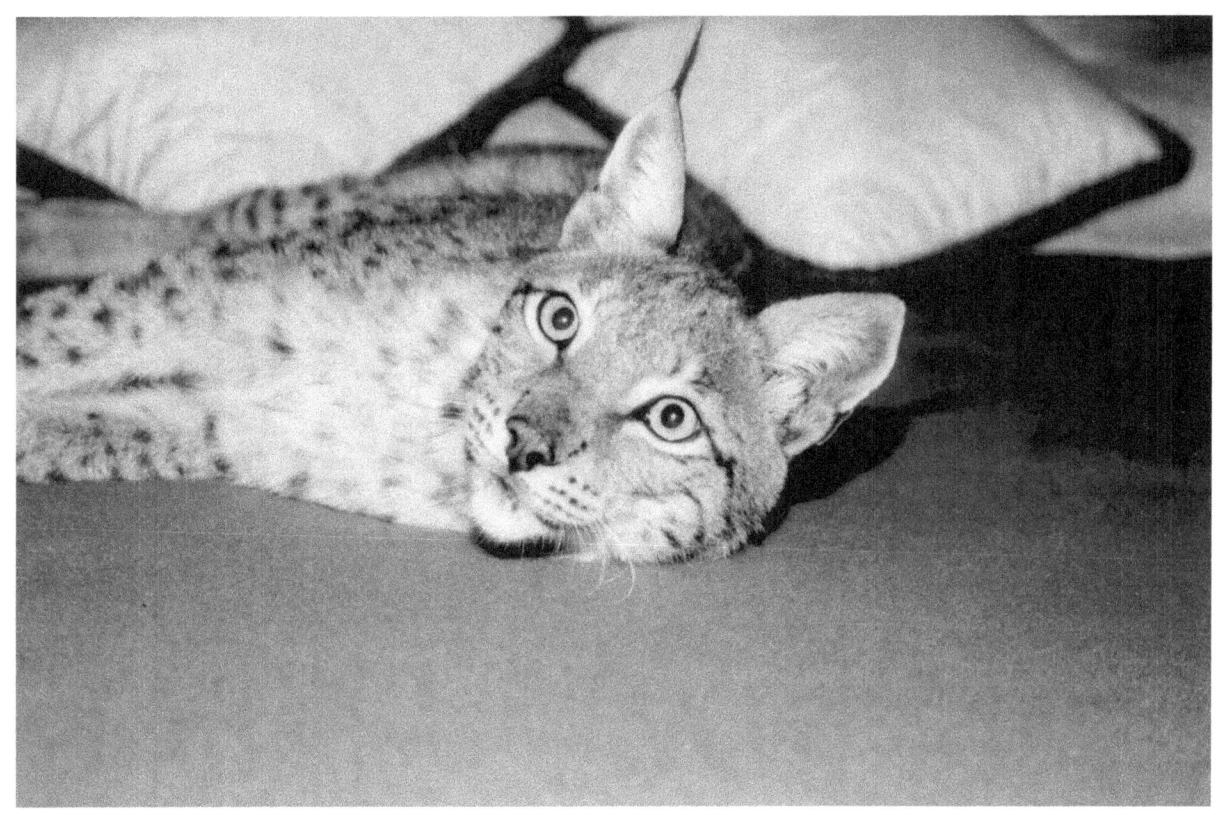

# HARRY
# THE GUARD CAT!

# Acknowledgements

I would like to thank the following people for their help and support in making this book a reality.

**Don & Nancy Clark**
Harry's owners and owners of the Midnight Contessa motor yacht aboard which all the photos were taken.

**Orange County Sheriff / Marina del Rey Sheriff's Dept.**
Sherman Block Sheriff for submitting photos of the Sheriff's boat and use permission.

And of course:

 # HARRY CAT

# About the Author

Roger Breterntiz has lived in southern California since 1972 coming from a little town in Illinois called Mahomet, where he grew up along the Sangamon River enjoying the outdoors as a young adventurer. He received a commercial art degree from Southern Illinois University in 1968, his BS education degree from Illinois State University in 1972, and after teaching art in the public school system in Rockford Illinois, came to sunny California settling in the Orange County area.

He enjoys playing and teaching tennis in the southern California area, along with many different sports such as skiing, archery, fishing, and trapshooting.

If you would like to get a better handle on organizing your life, your goals, gaining personal power, and using your mental powers to materialize those goals, you should check out his newest book, 2 years in the making appropriately called *WINNING: It's a lot more fun*. Just go to http://www.awinnersway.com/winning it can be purchased through amazon.com also, especially if you are OUT OF THE UNITED STATES (We do not ship outside the U.S.) Just put in the complete title, it comes up along with a Kindle version.

Roger also is a certified clinical Hypnotherapist and has his own line of self-improvement CDs that he creates in his recording studio, called Vector Studios where the DVD slide show for this book was conceived and produced. With it you can listen as you go through the book hearing all the music and sound effects as well as the professionally recorded voice over. It can be purchased on the web site http://www.vectorstudios.com/kidsstories . If you like the "Harry book" you will love the other 3 children's stories on audio CD (no pictures), Henry the Little Cactus, The Giraffe who Lost its Spots, and Wild Horse (A young Indian boy tames a great horse and saves his village). They can be played at home or in your auto.

If you like music with a country flair you should check out his album, "A Little Bit Country" on his web site: http://www.theotherband.us/rttaylor It has 8 up tempo tunes about life love, and having fun!

The book "Harry the Guard Cat" was just a fun project that turned into a great story for children that he hopes will bring lots of enjoyment for parents and children alike. Remember: Reading to your kids more, connects with your kids more. JUST DO IT!

Call for more info or to order- 949 542 7935

Roger would like to thank you all for your interest in Harry the Guard Cat and wishes you the best.

Roger W. Breternitz

www.ingramcontent.com/pod-product-compliance
Lightning Source LLC
Chambersburg PA
CBHW081843280526
45789CB00007B/2548